insight text guide

Anica Boulanger-Mashberg

Hatchet

Gary Paulsen

Copyright © Insight Publications 2022

First published in 2022.

Insight Publications Pty Ltd
3/350 Charman Road
Cheltenham VIC 3192
Australia
Tel: +61 3 8571 4950
Fax: +61 3 8571 0257
Email: books@insightpublications.com.au

www.insightpublications.com.au

Copying for educational purposes
The Australian *Copyright Act 1968* (the Act) allows a maximum of one chapter or 10% of this book, whichever is the greater, to be copied by any educational institution for its educational purposes provided that the educational institution (or the body that administers it) has given a remuneration notice to Copyright Agency under the Act.

For details of the Copyright Agency licence for educational institutions contact:

Copyright Agency
Tel: +61 2 9394 7600
Fax: +61 2 9394 7601
www.copyright.com.au

Copying for other purposes
Except as permitted under the Act (for example, any fair dealing for the purposes of study, research, criticism or review) no part of this book may be reproduced, stored in a retrieval system, or transmitted in any form or by any means without prior written permission. All inquiries should be made to the publisher at the address above.

A catalogue record for this book is available from the National Library of Australia

Gary Paulsens' Hatchet / Anica Boulanger-Mashberg

Anica Boulanger-Mashberg asserts the moral right to be identified as the author of this work.

ISBNs:
9781922525994 (print)
9781922771001 (digital)
9781922771018 (bundle: print + digital)

Cover design by Melisa Paredes

Printed in Australia by Ligare Book Printers

contents

Character map iv

Overview 1

About the author 1

Synopsis 2

Character summaries 3

Background & context 5

Genre, structure & language 9

Chapter-by-chapter analysis 17

Characters & relationships 33

Themes, ideas & values 43

Different interpretations 53

Questions & answers 57

Sample answer 66

References & reading 68

CHARACTER MAP

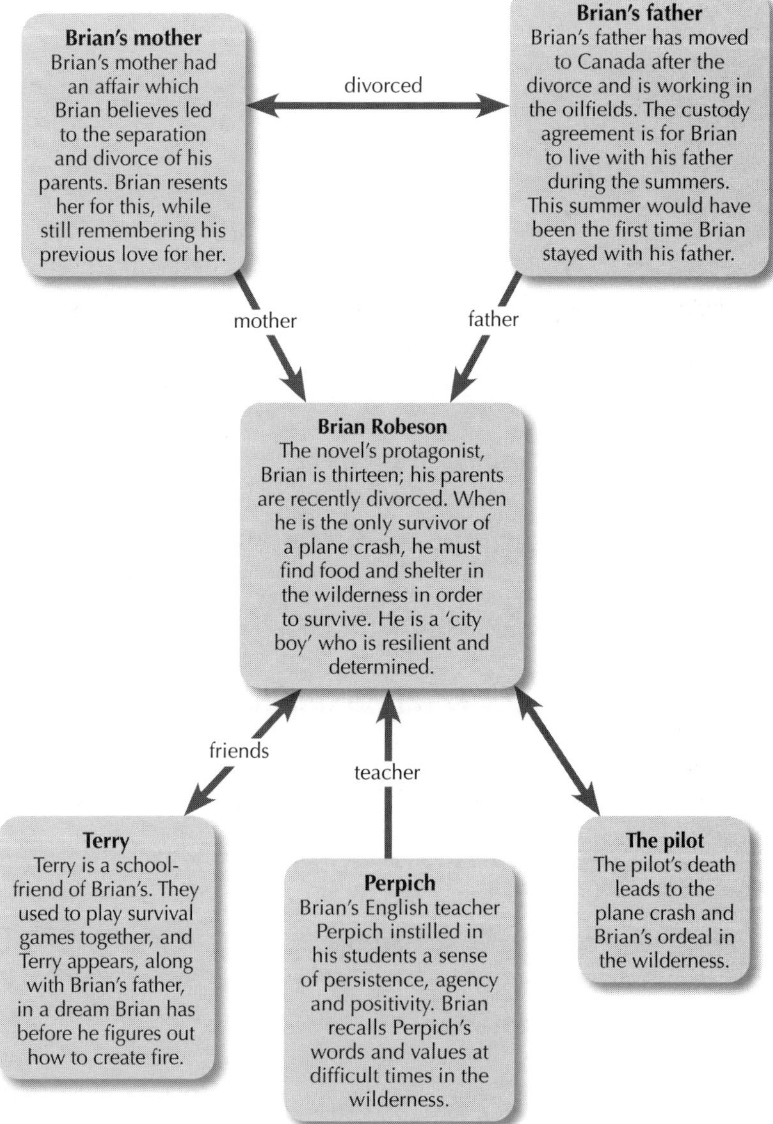

OVERVIEW

About the author

Gary Paulsen (1939–2021) was an exceptionally prolific American author who is perhaps best known for his series featuring Brian Robeson, beginning with *Hatchet* (1987). Paulsen led a life of extremely wide-ranging experiences after he began running away from home at around age twelve, when his family situation was unbearable and his very difficult relationships with his parents meant that living on his own was far preferable to living with his family. He worked in professions as wildly different as magazine editor and satellite technician, but had a particular affinity with the outdoors and the wilderness, and often found jobs that allowed him to indulge that preference. Many of his books feature outdoor adventure and survival stories, and many of those take inspiration from events and experiences in his own life. He was awarded the American Library Association's Margaret A. Edwards Award in 1997 for his contribution to young adult literature.

Paulsen wrote more than 200 books as well as short stories, hundreds of magazine articles and several plays. His works cover a vast range of genres including historical fiction and, under a pseudonym, Westerns, but some of his most returned-to subjects are the wilderness, survival and human life in nature. *Hatchet*, like two of Paulsen's other books, was a Newbery Honor winner. It has inspired a film (*A Cry in the Wild*, 1990), fanfiction, and (by more recent fans) Minecraft worlds and Roblox games.

Paulsen had little online presence and eschewed much of modern technology, preferring the challenges and rewards of a somewhat isolated life in wild landscapes away from cities and heavily populated areas. He had homes in several remote areas, including a cabin in rural Minnesota and a houseboat on the Pacific Ocean. Shortly before his death, he was still writing new novels, living on a ranch in New Mexico.

Synopsis

Thirteen-year-old Brian Robeson, whose parents are recently divorced, is flying in a single-engine plane from New York to Canada to spend his holidays with his father. He has been very upset by the separation, particularly as he had accidently discovered 'the Secret' leading to the divorce: his mother had been having an affair. His father still doesn't know, and Brian is tormented by the knowledge and the memory of seeing his mother with another man. Just as he is once again going over and over the events of the divorce in his mind, the pilot of the plane suffers a heart attack. Brian is forced to take over and manages to crash-land the plane into a lake in the dense Canadian wilderness over which they were flying. By chance, he has with him a hatchet his mother had given him before he got on the plane; she had intended him to use it in the woods with his father. This tool is central to his survival and allows him to build weapons, other tools and shelter.

Alone and trapped in the wilderness for most of the remainder of the book (until the final chapter), Brian gradually grows physically and mentally stronger with every hurdle he overcomes, and he feels more and more independent and confident. He suffers challenge after overwhelming challenge, and whenever he begins to feel comfortable – such as when he makes himself a bow and arrow and learns to catch fish in the lake – yet another disaster befalls him. Among other hardships, he copes with insect swarms and sunburn on top of his injuries from the plane crash; porcupine quills become embedded in his leg; his small food supply is eaten by a skunk that then sprays him; he is attacked by a moose; he loses most of his meagre belongings in a tornado; and he drops his hatchet in the lake and nearly drowns. During his almost two months alone, he learns to start a fire; catch fish, birds and rabbits for food; make tools; and construct shelter. In the process, he not only survives but begins, to some extent, to thrive and to appreciate his surroundings.

As the book concludes, Brian manages to dive into the wreckage of the plane and retrieve the emergency survival pack, which turns out to contain riches beyond imagination in his circumstances: food, a sleeping bag, tools and cooking implements, first-aid supplies, soap, a rifle and, crucially, an emergency transmitter. The day after he retrieves the pack, a plane – something he had wished for so ardently in the early days after the crash – detects the transmitter and arrives to rescue him, and the book ends with the bittersweet knowledge that, although he has been saved, he will be farewelling a world that, despite its incredibly punishing challenges, has become a home where he feels strong.

Character summaries

Brian Robeson

Brian is the protagonist and the only character present for most of the book. He is thirteen, and a 'city boy' who has little experience of the wilderness before the plane crash.

Brian's parents

Brian's mother and father divorced a month before the book begins, leaving Brian suspended in a shared custody arrangement between the two of them. His mother had an affair (about which only Brian knows), apparently precipitating the divorce, and his father is working in the Canadian oil fields.

Terry

Terry is a friend of Brian's; well before the plane crash, they played at wilderness survival together in the safety of the city, though it barely approximated what Brian experiences in reality.

Perpich

Perpich was an old English teacher of Brian's who had a focus on positivity. The memory of Perpich's teachings becomes a source of motivation for Brian in his struggle for survival.

The pilot

Brian never knows the name of the pilot whose heart attack causes the plane crash, and calls him 'Jim or Jake or something' (p.1); he is a very minor character and after the crash his only presence in the text is in the memories Brian has of him, and on the occasion when Brian dives into the wreck of the plane. In this scene, Brian is confronted underwater with the pilot's skull which has been almost entirely scoured by fish, and he has the horrifying realisation that the fish he has been eating have been feeding on the remains of the pilot.

BACKGROUND & CONTEXT

Geographical setting

Brian's plane crashes in an unspecified area of wilderness somewhere between Hampton (in New York state) and the Canadian oilfields where his father is working. It is logical that we as readers do not know exactly where Brian is, because he himself does not know. During the crash he has no idea how far the plane has drifted from its flight path, so there is no way to figure out where he has landed.

The plants and animals you encounter as you read the novel are evocative of this particular North American context, but many are also found in other places (examples include the porcupine, the moose, the beaver, the raspberries and the turtle). Thus the story is more about Brian's own journey and challenges in the wild than it is about the specific place in which he has landed. In some ways, the novel could take place just about anywhere: what is important is that he is exceedingly isolated from any kind of human settlement, and that he is alone – with the exception of the wild creatures.

Brian doesn't always know exactly what the wildlife and plants around him are. For example, he takes a chance on eating the 'gut cherries', he does not identify the fish he catches, and he knows the birds he hunts only as 'foolbirds'. But Paulsen uses very detailed physical descriptions to give readers a clear idea of the layout of the land around Brian – while the specific types of flora and fauna are not central to the story, the physical environment very much is. The shape and geography of the lake, the shape of the rock shelter Brian turns into a home, and the precise position of the plane in the water are all important in understanding Brian's exact challenges and achievements.

A key example is the paragraph describing Brian's shelter when he finds it:

> Using the sun and the fact that it rose in the east and set in the west, he decided that the far side was the northern side of the ridge. At one time in the far past it had been scooped by something, probably a glacier, and this scooping had left a kind of sideways bowl, back in under a ledge. It wasn't very deep, not a cave, but it was smooth and made a perfect roof and he could almost stand in under the ledge. He had to hold his head slightly tipped forward at the front to keep it from hitting the top. (p.46)

Here are some other examples of this type of detailed description.

- 'The lake stretched out slightly below him. He was at the base of the L, looking up the long part with the short part out to his right … He could see the reflections of the trees at the other end of the lake' (p.31).
- 'Above the door to the shelter, up the rock face about ten feet, was a small ledge that could make a natural storage place, unreachable to animals – except that it was unreachable to him as well' (p.108).
- '… he had cleaned away the whole side and top of the fuselage that stuck out of the water, had cut down into the water as far as he could reach and had a hole almost as big as he was, except that it was crossed and criss-crossed with aluminium – or it might be steel, he couldn't tell – braces and struts and cables' (p.144).

Author's biographical context

In *Hatchet*, Brian is forced into his wilderness retreat, coming to appreciate its isolation and intensity gradually as he becomes more and more adept at survival and at understanding and connecting with his environment. But for a young Paulsen, the wilderness was a retreat he actively sought, as it provided more stability and safety than his extremely difficult home life with parents who he described as 'drunks … awful' (Balaban 2021a) and 'brutal' (Sides 2006). He ran away from home regularly in order to escape the life that was damaging him, and his survival skills, already honed as a child in order to get through the early challenges of his mother's alcoholism, became high-level expertise when it came to living in the wild. Like Brian, he learned to hunt, fish and build shelter, as well as other survival skills such as using smoke to banish mosquitoes (Balaban 2021b). As well as facilitating his physical survival, these skills also became sources of emotional strength, as they allowed him to have a greater agency in the world than he had had as a small child when his mother was taking advantage of him, by forcing him to sing in bars in exchange for more alcohol for herself.

Paulsen's time in the wilderness also produced a longer-term psychological and vocational advantage for him, one that he would rely upon for decades into the future: his experiences provided the inspiration for many of his books. While, of course, the character of Brian in the book is not the same person as the author, they share much in common. In fact, in Paulsen's memoir, *Gone to the Woods* (2021), he writes in the third person, describing his life as though it were someone else's – almost re-creating himself as a character in a novel, as he does to an extent through Brian. In this way, the lines between Paulsen and his protagonists are sometimes blurred, and his narratives focus more on telling a shared story than on remaining either 'true' or 'fictional'.

Paulsen's tendency to merge real with imagined stories is not restricted to the Brian Robeson series, and can be quite explicit. For example, the novel *The Legend of Bass Reeves: Being the True and Fictional Account of the Most Valiant Marshal in the West* (2006) acknowledges, right up front in the title, Paulsen's focus on telling true stories through fictional lenses.

Historical setting

The historical setting is a component of any text. It is impossible for an author not to be influenced by the context of the world around them as they write, and if they are writing about an era other than the one in which they are living, this is also a significant element of the text. In this case, however, even though the book was written in the 1980s, there is little content that would date it. Being set in the wilderness, beyond the urban space of technology, fashion and social mores, *Hatchet* could be taking place in any number of unnamed eras. If the plane crashed today, certainly Brian might have had a mobile phone or some form of digital technology with him, but it would have been unlikely to survive the crash or, if it did, to function in the extremely remote wilderness. So in this case the historical setting of the book – either the historical context of the author or the historical setting of the narrative itself – would not be something you would spend much time discussing.

GENRE, STRUCTURE & LANGUAGE

Genre

Hatchet is a wilderness adventure novel for readers in the upper primary and early high school age group, focusing mainly on the individual physical challenges Brian faces, and on his coping resources and internal development. Although he is thirteen and therefore moving out of childhood towards early adulthood, his experiences in the book are not concerned with puberty, early relationships and navigating a social journey into an adult society – topics that are often the focus of young adult fiction. Likewise, fiction for younger readers frequently explores themes of developing identity, fitting in with peers, building relationships and interacting with school and family. In terms of subject matter, *Hatchet* doesn't fit neatly into the genres of middle grade or young adult fiction.

Brian's story is one that echoes the classical bildungsroman genre, in which the central character goes on a journey from (usually) childhood to some form of emotional or chronological maturity. Regardless of the fact that Brian is alone on his emotional journey while bildungsroman novels commonly chart characters' relationships with others, he reaches a level of wisdom and maturity in the novel, as his survival and triumphs over the intense demands of his ordeal bring him a sense of strength, confidence and independence he has never had before.

Structure

The narrative progresses chronologically from Brian's crash to his rescue, with only a few brief flashbacks. He moves swiftly from one trial to the next, giving the story a sense of immediacy which helps keep the reader engaged with his journey and his challenges, while maintaining the tension of each new adventure. The structure of events and resolutions becomes familiar as the novel progresses, with each of Brian's successes followed by a new trial for him to face.

The secondary plot is an extremely minor one, told in brief occasional flashbacks through Brian's intrusive memories of events. This story concerns his parents' divorce, particularly focusing on what Brian calls 'the Secret': his mother's affair before the marriage dissolved. This subplot takes place completely in the past, though his mother is present at the start of his journey, immediately before the plane flight.

Each chapter is structured around a particular event in Brian's ongoing survival bid. These usually consist of a challenge to be met; for example, crash-landing the plane, building a fire or securing various food sources. This pattern of challenge and success creates a forward momentum within each chapter. In addition, many of the chapters have a motif created by the repetition of words or phrases throughout. These motifs often provide us with information about Brian's mindset, including what particular stage of his journey he is undergoing. For example, in the first few chapters, Brian's preoccupation with the divorce and 'the Secret' indicates that he is still caught up in his life 'before', and is concerned with his past experiences and people who will gradually become less and less important to him. The recurring phrase: 'There were these things to do' (p.84, p.86, p.89) is another example of this kind of repetition, indicating the extent to which Brian needs to work to sustain himself. The subtext of the repetition is that this focus on work is necessary for Brian to avoid falling into a deep despair.

Language

The language choices in *Hatchet* mainly relate to descriptive prose, since there is almost no dialogue, and the language often reflects tangible experiences and the external surroundings rather than focusing on Brian's emotions or internal musings – though there are times when these are important too. The style of the description therefore helps set the tone for the whole novel.

Paulsen uses a mix of both concrete, precise writing and rich, sensory vocabulary to construct Brian's world, conveying in great detail the landscape and wildlife around him, and transporting readers to the isolated wilderness with all its sounds, smells and sensations. For example, when Brian is sprayed by the skunk, his experience is described in striking, intense sensory language:

> The thick sulphurous rotten odour filled the small room, heavy, ugly and stinking. The corrosive spray that hit his face seared into his lungs and eyes, blinding him. (p.105)

Elements Paulsen frequently describes vividly, using emotive language and figurative or sensory imagery, include the following.

Animals:

- '... thick, whining, buzzing masses of ... Mosquitoes and some small black flies ... All biting, chewing, taking from him' (p.29; sensory imagery and emotive language).
- 'A round-shaped fish, with golden sides, sides as gold as the sun' (p.102; simile).
- A bird is 'like a pear ... with a point on one end and a fat little body; a flying pear' (p.114; simile).

Food and water:

- '... he brought a cupped hand to his mouth and felt the cold lake water trickle past his cracked lips ... It was as if the water were more than water, as if the water had become all of life' (p.35; sensory imagery and simile).
- The 'stream of red liquid' from the raspberries he finds is 'sweet and tangy, like pop without the fizz' (p.62; simile).
- The raw turtle eggs 'had a greasy, almost oily taste ... his whole body seemed to convulse with it, but his stomach took it, held it, and demanded more' (p.82; sensory imagery and personification).
- The fish's 'skin crackled and peeled away and the meat inside was flaky and moist and tender' (p.102; sensory imagery).

Pain:

- 'A colour came that he had never seen before, a colour that exploded in his mind with the pain and he was gone, gone from it all … spiralling out into nothing' (p.24; metaphor).
- 'It was as if all the berries, all the pips had exploded in the centre of him, ripped and tore at him' (p.54; emotive language and simile).
- His leg feels 'as if a hundred needles had been driven into it' (p.63; simile).

In contrast, Paulsen often uses very concrete language to describe scenes of great distress and danger, and at times this choice of literal, straightforward words and phrases serves to heighten the impact of the descriptions of brutal incidents such as the tornado or the plane crash. By avoiding figurative language in these moments, the text focuses our attention on the physical experience and the intensity of what is happening to Brian. Examples include the following.

- 'He saw nothing but sensed blue, cold blue-green, and he raked at the seatbelt catch, tore his nails loose on one hand' (p.23).
- 'Mud filled his eyes, his ears, the horn boss on the moose drove him deeper and deeper into the bottom muck' (p.121; a 'boss' in this context describes a protuberance on an animal's body – although this moose is female and so does not have antlers, Paulsen is likely referring to the hard part of her forehead where, in a male moose, the antlers would connect to the skull).
- 'He felt a burning on his neck and reached up to find red coals there. He brushed those off, found more on his trousers, brushed those away, and the wind hit again' (p.125).

Additionally, concrete language choices can be used to contribute to a very distinct image of the landscape around Brian, which plays such a central role in the novel that it is vital that readers can imagine it clearly. In these phrases and sections, the text is very detailed, describing objects and places with careful attention to their shape, size and relationships with each other.

The following are some examples of such descriptions.

- 'In front of him lay the lake, blue and deep ... stretched out slightly below him. He was at the base of the L, looking up the long part with the short part out to his right' (p.31).
- 'For a good distance, perhaps two hundred yards, it was fairly clear. There were tall pines, the kind with no limbs until very close to the top ... but not too much low brush' (p.50).
- 'His leg was also back to normal, although he had a small pattern of holes – roughly star-shaped – where the quills had nailed him' (p.85).
- 'Only a short piece of the top of the fuselage, the plane's body towards the tail, was out of the water, just a curve of aluminium' (p.138).

While the figurative and the literal language choices differ in their ways of communicating ideas, the combination of both allows us to connect with the text by helping us to understand Brian's experiences and to see his surroundings in our mind's eye, and imagine his internal responses to them.

Repetition

Another distinctive language feature in the novel is the use of repetition. This is introduced powerfully in the first chapter, as Brian's memories of the divorce force themselves insistently into his mind. Note the repetition of one- or two-word paragraphs on page 2, as the painful ideas of 'divorce' and 'the Secret' churn over and over again through his thoughts. The word 'divorce' occurs several other times in this chapter too, indicating its significance for Brian. With the story's heavy emphasis on this part of Brian's life, we are just as shocked as he is by the sudden disaster of the plane crash, as we have been caught up in his preoccupation rather than focusing on his immediate situation.

This pattern of repetition occurs in later chapters too, such as in Chapter Eleven, which includes the sentence 'There were these things to do' (p.84, p.86, p.89) at the beginning, middle and end. The chapter also includes variations on the phrase, such as 'So there were things to do' (p.84) and 'Things to do' (p.86). In each case these variations form complete paragraphs that contrast with the longer surrounding paragraphs and, in this way, concentrate our attention on the repeated idea. In this chapter, the idea is of Brian finding ways to distract himself from his situation by focusing on his need to survive and to adapt to his surroundings. When you find such repetitions in a text, you can be certain that the writer wants you to pay particular attention to the idea, event or thoughts of the character.

Repetition plays this role at various stages of the novel, creating motifs that establish the mood or focus of the chapter or section. Given that there are few significant changes in scenery, chronology or character interaction, Paulsen uses other methods to create shifts in tone or situation. Such explicit repetition is one way of doing this. For example, the idea of Brian being 'not the same' (p.85, p.99) indicates to us that, in this central part of the narrative, the focus should be on Brian's growing strength and independence and his shift from being a 'city boy' (p.79) to being someone who can navigate his surroundings and take control of his own survival. The phrase 'city boy', in fact, is the subject of a different kind of repetition – one that isn't spread throughout a chapter, but used carefully to build up an image:

> City boy, he thought. Oh, you city boy with your city ways … City boy with your city ways sitting in the sand trying to read the tracks and not knowing, not understanding. (p.79)

In each of the three sentences above, Paulsen includes 'city boy' at or near the beginning, then adds further detail, elaborating on and delving deeper and deeper into the idea. The technique of beginning successive fragments, sentences or paragraphs with the same word or phrase is called *anaphora*, which is used to create emphasis. Paulsen uses a loose version of this strategy throughout the book. For example:

> And Brian saw it.
>
> Saw this thing that his mother did with the blond man. Saw the kiss that became the Secret that his father still did not know about … (p.55)

Here, each sentence uses repetition to provide us with more information about what Brian is thinking and remembering. As with the previous example, the repetition occurs three times. This is a literary device known as *tricolon*, which refers to three words, phrases or sentences that are parallel in some way (for example, in structure or length). The three sentences here increase in length and complexity – this is sometimes called a *tricolon crescens* or a 'rising tricolon', meaning that each phrase or sentence builds on and extends the last. The choice of three is not coincidental: three is often identified as a powerful number in artistic representation, as it is generally considered the fewest number of components required to create a pattern. By creating patterns of language, Paulsen shapes and directs our attention to particular ideas.

Narrative voice

Hatchet is told from the third-person limited point of view, so the perspective is at once removed from the protagonist yet also intimately tied to him. This allows us to both observe Brian alongside his context, viewing him as an element in the environment, and also have a close understanding of his experiences and feelings.

The third person ('she', 'he', 'they' etc.) typically serves to distance the reader from the protagonist/s of a story, and encourages the reader to see events and the characters' actions and experiences from a broader perspective than first- or second-person narratives. This can allow readers to draw connections or reach conclusions that the characters themselves do not (or cannot). It can also allow readers to form their own interpretations of the events and ideas within a text, since they are not necessarily tied to one character's perspective.

The third-person limited perspective uses third-person pronouns, but also allows access to a focal character's internal experiences, rather than simply reporting their behaviour from the outside. For example, although *Hatchet* is not told in the first person, we know intimately what Brian is feeling during events such as the crash or his dive into the submerged plane near the conclusion of the novel. His internal experiences are described in great detail, drawing us closely into the narrative.

Limiting the narrator's knowledge to that of one single character's perspective and inner world can encourage readers to empathise particularly with that character and their views and values, which can in turn shape overall interpretations of a text. In *Hatchet*, however, as there are no characters other than the protagonist for the bulk of the story, the use of this narrative point of view allows us to take a step back and to view the wilderness almost as a character itself – Brian's interactions are with the plants, animals, weather and terrain around him and so these become his key relationships in the text.

Although the narrative is in the third person, the text frequently uses Brian's first-person thoughts and internal monologue. For example:

> I am Brian Robeson. I have been in a plane crash. I am going to find some food. I am going to find berries. (p.50)

The use of the first person 'I' within these phrases alerts us to the fact that we are directly accessing his thoughts and self-talk. Although Paulsen does not use quotation marks to distinguish this content from the surrounding third-person text, he does use *dialogue tags* or *attribution tags* – phrases such as 'he thought' – to transition between Brian's perspective and the narrator's third-person descriptions. Shifting between these two modes allows the reader to develop a strong relationship with the protagonist.

CHAPTER-BY-CHAPTER ANALYSIS

Chapter One (pp.1–10)

Summary: *Brian is a passenger in a light plane; he remembers his parents' divorce and his mother bringing him to the airport; the pilot suffers a fatal heart attack.*

Brian, a dejected thirteen-year-old, has resigned himself to the fact that he has to fly in a small plane to stay with his father for the summer after his parents' recent divorce and custody arrangements. As the only passenger in the plane he has little to do to pass the time and, with nothing to distract him, 'The thinking started' (p.2), as he revisits the distress of the divorce and, particularly, of his unique and upsetting position of knowing 'the Secret' (which we will later learn is that his mother was having an affair).

The pilot lets him have a turn at flying the plane, telling him that 'it's not as complicated as it looks' (p.3) and that it 'just takes learning. Like everything else' (p.4) – an idea that is upheld throughout the book. Brian is at first reluctant but briefly enjoys discovering that he can in fact do it. This foreshadows his progress later in the novel, as he is at first helpless in the wild but steadily learns how to keep himself alive.

Brian reflects on the events leading up to the trip – first the court's custody decision and then his mother driving him to the airport. The tension between Brian and his mother is painful, as Brian can't forget 'the Secret' and is resentful of it, though his nostalgia for 'the tenderness in her voice that she had when he was small' reminds him of his past closeness to her (p.7). As a gift, she gives him the hatchet that he forgets about and boards the plane with – a tool that will facilitate his survival after the crash.

At the end of the chapter, the pilot suffers a heart attack and collapses, and Brian realises that he will have to somehow survive on the plane alone.

Key point

The repetition of the word 'alone' in the final three short paragraphs at the end of this chapter foreshadows the rest of the book, where Brian's aloneness is the most significant element of his adventure.

Q What do you think is the most noteworthy moment in this chapter? Why?

Chapter Two (pp.11–20)

Summary: *Brian flies the plane on his own and tries to contact help.*

Realising the pilot is dead, Brian does his best to control the plane, but knows nothing about the controls and dials or what to do and, panicking, he takes the pilot's headset and attempts to contact help. After briefly making CB radio contact with someone and beginning to tell them his situation, he suddenly loses signal and knows he is on his own. He makes a plan for crash-landing into a lake when the plane runs out of fuel, and the chapter concludes as the engine dies in midair. In this chapter we see a glimpse of the Brian to come: no matter how scared he is and how unfamiliar the challenges facing him are, he never gives up and instead finds ways to problem-solve and survive.

Q How is the language in this chapter different from the language in the previous chapter?

Chapter Three (pp.21–4)

Summary: *The plane crashes through trees and into a lake; Brian manages to escape the plane and avoid drowning.*

Already, though he doesn't realise it, Brian has started to adapt into the necessary survival mode, planning his crashlanding despite his extreme distress. But he is also aided by a stroke of luck – a lake happens to appear before he is forced to crash the plane into solid forest. This combination of persistence and good luck will help him throughout his time in the wild, although he also experiences more than his fair share of very bad luck, such as later when the tornado hits.

His shocking crash is described in visceral detail, with no sugar-coating of the terrifying experience as the plane smashes through the trees to the water, and then as he fights to pull himself out of the underwater plane and avoid drowning. Emotive words and phrases such as 'blinded ... slammed ... smashing', 'tight animal screams', 'shattered', 'clawed' and 'ripping' generate an atmosphere of drama and trauma (p.23). The language creates a vivid image of the pain he is suffering, and this no-holds-barred approach to describing his struggles is maintained throughout the book.

Q How believable do you find Brian's first feat of survival?

Chapter Four (pp.25–33)

Summary: *Brian has a flashback to seeing his mother in a car with another man; he regains consciousness and drags himself out of the lake; he feels dazed from the accident; he is attacked by a swarm of mosquitoes; he registers his surroundings.*

In a digression from the horror scenes of the plane crash and before the narrative of his disaster recovery begins, Brian remembers discovering that his mother was having an affair. The placement of this memory, between the scenes of the crash and his injury-ridden aftermath, suggests that his discovery of his mother's infidelity caused him an emotional devastation similar to the physical devastation he is currently experiencing. By including a memory of the past here, Paulsen interrupts the description of Brian's current experience, bringing tension to the narrative as we wait to see how Brian has survived.

Once Brian starts emerging from his apparently concussed state, he begins to catalogue his injuries and similarly catalogue his surroundings. He notices animals, birds, plants and the sounds of the forest. He realises how different this world is to the 'grey and black of the city' he is familiar with (p.33). This is his first early connection to his environment – one he will later come to deeply value.

Q What do you think Brian means by 'if you keep walking back from good luck … you'll come to bad luck' (p.32)?

Chapter Five (pp.34–44)

Summary: *Brian quenches his thirst with water from the lake; he thinks about when he might be rescued; he remembers the 'positivity' philosophy of a past schoolteacher, and thinks about how he could survive for a few days.*

Brian consciously begins to assess his situation. He considers what has happened and thinks about the possibility that he will be rescued soon – 'probably … today' (p.37), or 'maybe not tomorrow, but soon. Soon. Soon' (p.43). He tries to reassure himself of this and yet at the same time he evaluates the dangers of the situation and environment (from hunger to wolves) and begins to take stock of the resources around him that could ensure his survival, knowing (though trying to avoid thinking about it) that 'they might not find him for a long time' and, in fact, 'might never find him' (p.42). But he does not allow himself to dwell on this terrifying prospect; rather, he relies on a memory of Perpich, one of his past English teachers, who instilled in his students the importance of 'being positive, thinking positive, staying on top of things' (p.39).

Perpich's philosophy is one of few parts of Brian's past that he brings into his experiences in the forest, and it is something he returns to at some of his low points. Here, he uses the ideas of positivity and motivation to avoid descending into deep panic and despair, remembering – even just for a moment – Perpich's words: 'You are your most valuable asset. Don't forget that. *You* are the best thing you have' (p.40). Although this does not particularly inspire Brian at this point, it is one of the central lessons he comes to learn by the end of the novel, when he has become a stronger and more independent person than he had ever been in the past – resourceful and resilient, and capable of survival in the most challenging of situations.

Q What is the significance of the moment of 'complete silence' Brian experiences on page 40?

Chapter Six (pp.45–53)

Summary: *Brian remembers playing games with Terry; he finds the overhang that will become his shelter; he finds and eats berries; he builds a front for the overhang.*

The chapter begins with Brian's memories of innocent survival games he had once played with his friend Terry. Their 'fooling around' (p.45) during that time is contrasted significantly with the reality Brian is experiencing, indicating that the innocent security of his past life has been corrupted by the trauma he has just undergone, as well as by the challenges he knows lie ahead. He thinks longingly of the resources they had imagined they would have, and yet he doesn't break down at this point but rather recognises some 'good luck' (p.46), both in having survived the landing and in finding the cave-like shelter. He brainstorms his options and focuses on figuring out how to find food to keep himself alive. His discovery of the berries and his construction of a protective door for the shelter show how quickly he is beginning to tune in to his surroundings and work hard at being resourceful in order to protect himself. Though he still expects to be found within several days, there are hints of how he might survive if such a rescue doesn't eventuate.

Q How would you describe Brian's mood in this chapter? How does it differ from that in the previous chapters?

Chapter Seven (pp.54–62)

Summary: *Brian is sick from the 'gut cherries'; he finds raspberries; he sees a bear.*

Directly contrasting with Brian's apparent success in the previous chapter, where we see him finding food and shelter for himself and therefore showing agency in his survival, this chapter begins with his terrible distress and physical illness resulting from the naive mistake of eating too many of what he calls the 'gut cherries'.

Key point

Brian's physical pain is linked, in this scene, with his persistent emotional pain relating to his mother's affair. As his strength and independence in the forest gradually increase, his thoughts of his mother and 'the Secret' decrease in frequency.

Although Brian has still not considered that he may be in the forest for much longer than the few days he hopes for, he takes himself by surprise when he thinks of the shelter as 'home' (p.58). He has learned quickly from his mistake with the gut cherries and, although he does plan to continue eating them (much more carefully), he also goes on a search for more food. When he finds the raspberries and eats them until he feels full, he does not 'gorge or cram more down', showing, again, how quickly he is learning from his errors and adapting to his surroundings (p.59).

Q Why does Brian consider his tears to be 'wasted tears' (p.56)?

Chapter Eight (pp.63–9)

Summary: *Brian is injured by a porcupine and must remove the quills; he realises that he can make sparks with his hatchet and thus will be able to create fire.*

As is the pattern in much of the book – a pattern Brian comes to recognise – a positive experience is closely followed by a negative one, as he swings between strength and vulnerability. As he puts it, 'So fast things change ... in just a moment it was all different' (p.64), reflecting on the unpredictability of the wild. This time, Brian's shelter is invaded during the night by a porcupine, some of whose quills become painfully embedded in Brian's leg. After this terrifying and excruciating incident, Brian learns what he considers 'the most important rule of survival, which was that feeling sorry for yourself didn't work' (p.65).

Paulsen makes use of foreshadowing in this chapter in the passing mention of the hatchet making sparks as it hits the stone wall (p.63). Readers will likely see this as a revelation of how Brian could start a valuable fire for himself. Brian, however, is so distracted by fear and pain that he does not register what has happened until much later, after he has a dream of fire – his subconscious trying to help him by reminding him about the sparks – and realises what he can do with the hatchet. This is an example of dramatic irony, where the audience realises something that the character does not yet know.

Q How does the text support Brian's idea that 'feeling sorry for yourself' doesn't work?

Q Why do you think it is Brian's father and Terry who try to communicate with him in his dream?

Chapter Nine (pp.70–5)

Summary: *Brian lights a fire.*

The chapter goes into great detail about Brian's efforts and eventual success in creating fire. The effect is that we are closely invested in the activity and empathise with Brian, almost as if we were creating the fire ourselves and making the discoveries along with him. There is a bittersweet note at the end of the chapter, however, when he realises 'there was nobody' for him to share his achievement and pride with (p.75). (Later, when he first catches a fish, he 'felt his throat tighten, swell, and fill with pride at what he had done', p.102, and seems not to feel any need to share that success with anyone else.) His thoughts turn once again to his parents and 'the Secret', a distress he is still unable to reconcile, even (and perhaps especially) in a moment of success. It is not often in the text that Brian feels lonely for human contact – his desires and needs are generally more practical and pragmatic.

Q Why do you think Brian's emotions about his family are so strong at the end of this chapter?

Chapter Ten (pp.76–83)

Summary: *Brian cuts and stores firewood; he discovers a nest of turtle eggs; he eats six of the eggs.*

In this chapter, Brian keeps the fire going and works hard at finding, cutting and carrying firewood. He thinks that 'for the first time since the crash ... he might be getting a handle on things', planning active survival strategies rather than relying on minimal or passive ones (p.78). At the same time, though, he observes, as one might see from the outside, a certain naivety regarding his new existence in the wild. While trying to understand the tracks in the sand, he recognises that in many ways he is still very much a 'city boy with ... city ways' and that he still has much to learn (p.79). He concludes that 'he must change' – not just that he must learn, but that he must, at a core level, *change* who he is in order to be *able* to learn (p.79).

When he discovers the nest of turtle eggs, Brian is thrilled to have at last found something other than berries to eat, but also repulsed at having to eat the eggs raw because, despite having created fire, he has nothing to cook on – the battle for survival is never-ending and he barely has time to celebrate one success before he meets his next challenge.

His hunger overrides his fear and he devours six eggs before forcing himself to save the rest, then realises that he has been planning ahead and, for a moment, has forgotten about imminent rescue. This illustrates his growing acceptance that he cannot rely on a potential rescue and may have to find ways to support himself in the longer term.

Q Brian thinks a lot about change in this chapter. In what ways has he already changed from the boy he was at the beginning of the book?

Chapter Eleven (pp.84–9)

Summary: *Brian continues cutting wood to refuel the fire; he discovers there are fish in the lake.*

Brian realises that by keeping busy he can take his mind off the emotional trauma of the crash and his worries about being rescued. Luckily, to survive in the forest there are plenty of things he can and must do, many of which are physically taxing and very time-consuming, such as keeping himself supplied with wood for the fire. Echoing his thoughts in the previous chapter, Brian evaluates significant changes in himself: in his body (such as his weight and his skin tone) and 'in the way he was' (p.85). It's not just that he has found strategies to survive (such as lighting the fire and picking berries); he is in the process of becoming a different kind of person – someone who relates intimately to his surroundings rather than taking everything for granted. He is more attentive to sensory stimuli such as noise, understanding what particular sounds mean, and he can see things in more detail than before – 'truly see ... not just notice it as he used to' (p.85). This recognition of the ways in which he has changed is linked to his next success: his realisation that he should be able to feed himself with fish from the lake.

Q What evidence can you find of the 'change' Brian is seeing in himself?

Chapter Twelve (pp.90–6)

Summary: *Brian makes a spear, and starts working on making a bow and arrow; he hears a plane and lights his signal fire but the plane is gone.*

Brian is working hard both mentally and physically, figuring out how to make a bow and arrow and thinking about how he might catch not just fish but perhaps birds. But in the midst of this optimistic flurry of activity, his hopes are brutally dashed when he doesn't manage to catch the attention of a plane. In many ways this is the most hopeless we have seen him: he 'could not play the game without a dream … He was alone and there was nothing for him' (p.96).

Key point

The fish spear is 'more than just a tool' (p.91), just as Brian's survival in the wild is not only about food and physical safety (though these are primary) but also about something deeper. The spear represents his growing maturity. Note that he is not able to use it effectively yet – this symbolises his ongoing journey.

Q What do you think is meant by 'a hunger that made him look for things, see things' (p.92)?

Chapter Thirteen (pp.97–103)

Summary: *Brian sees a wolf; he reflects on his deep depression and recovery after the plane had passed; he has success catching fish with his bow and arrow.*

This chapter holds another key turning point for Brian, forty-seven days after the crash. Frequently he compares himself to 'the old Brian', who was 'weak', and notes the fact that 'the plane passing changed him … He was not the same and would never be again' (p.100). As well as these subjective feelings, there is concrete evidence of how he has changed while living in the forest: for example, his ability to recognise subtle details in his environment that alert him to danger (as when he senses the wolf, p.98). Further evidence includes his increased capacity and confidence to source food for himself as he learns to catch fish, having resourcefully made himself a bow and arrow and worked through the challenge of how to use it.

This chapter presents a kind of rebirth, as Brian recalls sinking to an unprecedented and suicidal low, but then surviving the night and becoming 'new' (p.100). The notion of renewal appears fairly frequently throughout the text, as Brian overcomes challenge after challenge. But this moment, following the plane's passing, is particularly powerful.

Key point

Brian attempts suicide with his own hatchet. It is perhaps ironic that his one tool, the one useful thing he had with him, is not only what he constantly turns to for survival, but also what he turns to for the *opposite* when he is at his very lowest point of desperation.

Q What does Brian's experience when he sees the wolf symbolise?

Chapter Fourteen (pp.104–10)

Summary: *Brian is sprayed by a skunk; he reconstructs his shelter and makes a food shelf; he builds a pen to store live fish.*

Picking up on a word he used several times in the previous chapter, Brian again reiterates that he has made many 'mistakes' in his struggle for survival – the word often forms a full paragraph on its own (p.104, p.106, p.108, p.109). This serves to emphasise not only the key idea of mistakes, but also the corresponding idea of overcoming and learning from mistakes. It is Brian's persistence that is keeping him alive, and he is aware that mistakes can have a great cost, such as when he loses all his eggs to the skunk because he hasn't protected them properly.

It is symbolic that in order to rebuild his shelter into a stronger and more enduring home, Brian begins by 'tearing it down' (p.107). This reflects the way in which the 'new' and stronger Brian has emerged after the safety of his past life, as well as his old habits and complacency, have been destroyed by the crash. The text suggests that sometimes, improvement requires the destruction of what already exists.

When he comes up with the idea of keeping a supply of fish alive in the water, Brian begins to move beyond a simple subsistence existence (scavenging for food for every meal): 'It wasn't just keeping from starving – it was trying to save ahead, think ahead' (p.110). This points to yet another transition in his thinking – from simply surviving in the moment to building longer-term infrastructure to sustain his survival.

Q What does Brian believe about mistakes?

Chapter Fifteen (pp.111–18)

Summary: *Brian learns to catch the foolbirds for food; he cooks and eats his first foolbird.*

This chapter again illustrates the pattern of successes and challenges for Brian: as soon as he has solved one problem, he is faced by another. Here, he must first figure out how to spot the birds before they fly away, then how to hunt them (failing with his bow and arrow before trying with his spear), then how to cook and prepare them.

Once again he finds that his 'friend' and 'guard', the fire (p.74), saves him. Not only does it keep him warm, protect him from mosquitoes (p.77) and allow him to cook, it now also keeps flies away from his food (p.117). We are reminded of how far he has come since his first vulnerable day when he was nearly devoured by mosquitoes after the crash.

Q Why do you think Brian's 'First Meat' (p.118) tastes better to him than anything he has ever eaten before (including the other foods he has found so far in the woods)?

Chapter Sixteen (pp.119–29)

Summary: *Brian is violently attacked by a moose; a tornado destroys most of his shelter.*

We are again reminded that Brian 'was not the same, would not be the same again' as his survival in the forest continues to challenge and strengthen him (p.119). With his new ability to tune in to his sensory input and recognise danger before he has even consciously registered it ('later he would not know why he started to turn', p.121), Brian sees the moose just before it attacks him. The moose attack, one of the many violent incidents in the novel, is presented in vivid sensory detail designed to intimately immerse the reader in the terrifying experience. Emotive words such as 'sputtered', 'sucking', 'fighting', 'charged', 'slamming', 'screamed' and 'hammered', along with repetition (particularly of the word 'insane'), convey the intensity of the incident (pp.121–2), and Brian's resulting injury is yet another reminder of how vulnerable he is, even as his survival skills continue to improve.

Close on the heels of the frightening bodily attack, the tornado arrives, destroying Brian's shelter in much the same way the moose almost destroyed his person. Again the emotive word choices contribute to the evocative description of this frightening experience: 'whipped', 'tearing', 'snapping' and 'slamming' (pp.125–6). After the storm, Brian feels as though he's lost everything – 'I am back to nothing … back to where I was when I crashed' (p.126) – and this is illustrated symbolically by the return of the mosquito swarms in the new absence of the fire. The storm has stripped him of all the progress he had made. And yet, 'there is a difference now', in that he has changed, grown, learned and become more 'tough' (p.127) than the boy who landed in the lake in the crash.

Key point

Remarkably, one of the most destructive incidents of Brian's time in the forest catalyses one of the most constructive parts of his journey. The partial re-emergence of the plane from the lake leads to his ultimate success in recovering the survival pack.

Q What is the most vivid image for you in Chapter Sixteen? Why?

Chapter Seventeen (pp.130–9)

Summary: *Brian repairs the damage to his home after the storm; he builds the raft and pushes it out to the plane.*

With determination, Brian goes about restoring his fire and shelter, and finding food. Despite his injuries, the setback has not cast him into the depression he felt after the plane passed him in Chapter Twelve. At this point in the novel, he has more skills than he had at each previous disaster, and knows that he can rebuild the security he had achieved for himself. He also shows his maturity, knowing that he needs to catch fish to feed himself before trying to get to the plane, despite his excitement and desire to go immediately.

For the remainder of the chapter, Brian labours over creating the raft, then in the morning exerts himself swimming with it out to the plane, and evaluates the situation, investigating the plane and brainstorming how he might be able to get into it. He exhibits his persistence and his commitment to problem-solving even when the situation seems impossible.

Key point

Yet another indication of Brian's growth is that he has moved on from seeing only terror and danger in the landscape around him, and while waiting for the next day when he can attempt the trip to the plane, he sees 'almost unbelievable beauty' as the sunset 'exploded the sky, just blew it up with the setting colour' (p.137). He has learned to appreciate his surroundings, and has also physically sustained himself to a point where he is able to think about something beyond pure survival.

Q Why do you think Brian doesn't give up after the storm?

Chapter Eighteen (pp.140–8)

Summary: *Brian drops his hatchet into the lake and dives to retrieve it; he cuts his way into the plane; he finds the survival pack and sees the pilot's skull; he takes the pack to shore.*

Immediately after Brian's triumphant discovery that he can cut through the plane's aluminium with his hatchet, he accidentally drops it: a devastating mistake given it is his one tool and the thing he has relied on more than almost anything else during his time since the crash. His 'self-pity' is brief, however, and he sets about finding a way to retrieve the hatchet, dismissing his own 'carelessness' and 'stupidity' in favour of finding a solution (p.141). Although he considers the mistake 'the kind of thing [he] would have done before', the difference is that now he has the resilience and physical strength to recover from it (p.141).

After his extraordinary feat of retrieving the hatchet from the bottom of the lake, Brian does not pause to congratulate himself, just as he had not paused for any significant amount of time to criticise himself after making the mistake. Instead, he gets straight on with the task at hand, working hard to get himself into the plane. Despite his misgivings about the danger of the situation, he reasons that the plane has not yet sunk so is likely to stay in position while he dives inside it. He manages to find the bag, then drags it out of the plane and rafts it to shore.

Q 'The hatchet was, had been him' (p.141). Does Brian place too much importance on the hatchet? Give reasons for your answer.

Chapter Nineteen (pp.149–54)

Summary: *Brian explores everything in the pack; he cooks a meal using the freeze-dried food packets; a rescue plane arrives.*

Brian opens the pack and marvels at all the 'presents' it contains – things that would have made his survival so much easier (p.150). Yet when he holds the rifle (a tool that could have been useful on countless recent occasions) it 'changed him … and he wasn't sure he liked the change very much' (p.150). This is the first time that a change in Brian has not represented positive growth and development. Instead, it almost takes him backwards, to an existence dependent on things other than his own resourcefulness, care and effort. He recognises the gun as something that disrupts the natural relationship between humans and their surroundings – a relationship he has come to deeply value. Similarly the lighter, while it makes starting the fire much simpler, makes him feel uneasy because it 'somehow removed him from where he was, what he had to know' (p.151). Finding the incredible 'riches' (p.149) in the pack brings very mixed, 'up and down' feelings for Brian (p.151).

Key point

As he did initially with the gut cherries and later with the fish (and partly with the turtle eggs, although he managed to control himself on that occasion), Brian decides to gorge on the food, planning to treat himself before he settles down to more sensible rationing. This shows two different sides of Brian – his passionate and impulsive side, and his careful, sensible and patient side.

Just as he's eating the first 'real' food he's had in months, giving him vivid flashbacks to his mother's cooking and his life before the crash, a rescue plane appears, as if summoned by his thoughts of home. He welcomes the pilot, 'not quite knowing yet that it was over' (p.154). For the reader, too, it is hard to imagine that Brian's adventure has ended so abruptly.

Q What do you think Paulsen wants us to feel in the last paragraph of the novel?

CHARACTERS & RELATIONSHIPS

Brian

Key quotes

'He had to do something to help himself.' (p.44)

'Right now I'm all I've got.' (p.44)

'Keep it simple. I am Brian Robeson. I have been in a plane crash. I am going to find some food. I am going to find berries.' (p.50)

'I am not the same, he thought … He did not know when the change started, but it was there …' (p.85)

'I am full of tough hope.' (p.103)

In this novel, Brian's character is not necessarily established in the ways you might expect. There is little description of his appearance, for example (other than when it relates to his physical injuries and his condition after the crash), and we know little of his past apart from his response to his parents' marriage dissolving. Instead, we need to focus on several main aspects of the text in order to form a picture of who Brian is.

Actions over dialogue

Brian has brief exchanges with others at the beginning and end of the book – with the pilot who dies and with the pilot who rescues him – but these are superficial and very short. The only other dialogue is either in his memory, such as his discussion with his mother before the flight, or is one-sided when he speaks out loud in the forest, such as when he first builds a fire and cries out 'Fire! … I've got fire!' and then addresses the fire itself: 'Hello, fire' (p.74). Occasionally this one-sided conversation takes the form of direct speech to animals, such as when he says, 'Get out of here' to the skunk (p.105). At other times he articulates a thought he is having ('Too many gut cherries', p.55; 'I wonder', p.109), but this is thinking aloud rather than conducting dialogue. As dialogue is a key element through which readers learn about characters' personalities, needs and desires – either from the ways in which characters speak with one another, or from what others say to or about them – we need to use other means to discover these things about Brian.

Instead of dialogue, then, we need to turn to action to learn about who Brian really is. Often, a simple action can tell us a lot about a character. The following are some examples of Brian's actions and what they tell us about him.

- After Brian recovers from the initial trauma of the crash, he lays out his belongings and takes stock of what items he has (pp.39–40). This shows that Brian is logical and methodical, evaluating the details of his situation even under great stress.
- Brian sometimes vomits from shock or horror, as well as in response to food he should not have eaten (p.20, p.24, p.35, p.54, p.146). However, he always recovers quickly and is not distressed by it; this shows that although his body is sometimes vulnerable at a basic physiological level, he is not often distressed or weakened psychologically by it.
- He eats the first berries he finds (p.51). This reminds us of his desperation – he is absolutely starving and responding to his basic human needs. However, it also suggests that he can be (at least in the early part of the book) somewhat naive. He does not consider whether the berries are safe, and his illness that night (p. 54) reinforces the fact that he has taken a risk without thinking about it.
- He pulls the porcupine quills out of his leg (p.65). Brian knows what he needs to do to take care of his injury, and he does so almost immediately – this indicates his decisiveness and strength in overcoming his own pain.
- He keeps developing his fish spear after it initially fails (pp.90–1), eventually making a bow and arrow and realising he needs to aim slightly below where the fish appear to be in the water (pp.101–2).

This reveals his capacity for persistence and problem-solving. These qualities are also shown in many of the other strategies he uses to refine his survival techniques, such as creating and keeping the fire going.

Brian's thoughts

Another way we can deduce information about Brian's character is through his inner monologue. While the book is written in the third person ('he', 'him') rather than the first ('I', 'me'), we are still privy to much of what Brian is thinking because it is conveyed to us directly; for example, 'I'm tough where it counts' (p.127). We have close access to his thoughts and subjective experience (since the narrative perspective is third-person limited), and this allows us to see his own perception of himself. In many texts, this would be only part of the picture, as other characters would perceive the protagonist in different ways, and interactions with others would indicate whether the protagonist's actual personality matched their own view of themselves. However, the only information we are ever provided with in *Hatchet* is Brian's thoughts and memories, and his direct experiences and resulting perception of himself. Since there is no source of contradiction, we must assume that Brian's perception of himself is an accurate representation of who he is.

Brian has a strong sense of self. He is very in tune with his own thoughts, needs and capacities, and is capable of monitoring and evaluating his own behaviour. This is particularly notable on the many occasions in which he observes that he has changed and is changing, and is not the 'city boy' (p.79) he was before the crash. He notices and assesses his own actions, mistakes and successes, and presents a clear picture of what motivates him (primarily survival), how he makes decisions (logically and with commitment) and what moves him (early in the book, his anger and distress about his mother's affair, then his physical trauma, then eventually his own strength).

At the same time that he recognises the changes in himself, he also works hard to hold on to his identity as he knows it. Along his journey of development, he still reminds himself of who he is and what he knows, beginning with the simplest of concrete facts: 'My name is Brian Robeson and I am thirteen years old' (p.36) and 'I am Brian Robeson' (p.50). He needs to make sure that he does not lose himself in this new and challenging environment.

Brian's inward-turning focus and self-awareness reflect both the setting and the central idea of survival alone in the wilderness. There are no distractions for him from any other humans; all he has to focus on is his need to survive, and his assessment of his own character. It is rare for him to even think about his relationships with others (apart from in brief memories), and when such thoughts do intrude – primarily via his persistent feelings about his parents' separation – it is mostly in the earlier parts of the book, and they occur less frequently as he spends more and more time alone. One of the few times he acknowledges his feelings about having been severed from his past existence is right at the end of the book when he realises he has 'missed music, missed sound, missed hearing another voice' (p.151). Notably, this is only prompted by the presence of the survival pack – something belonging to that other world and not to the one he has been living in.

You would probably find it easy to respond immediately to the following questions about Brian. Is he:

- energetic or lazy?
- bold or timid?
- emotional or detached?
- persistent or half-hearted?
- self-aware or oblivious?
- physically strong or weak?

But how do we justify these interpretations? For each of the dot points above, find at least one piece of evidence from the text to support your opinion or interpretation. Evidence might include quotations, events, and Brian's self-realisations or self-analyses. Your answers and examples will help you to build up a justified understanding of the character.

Relationships

Just as dialogue is largely absent from the book, relationships are also extremely limited. Relationships in texts normally enable us to glean information about characters and their motivations. In this text, Brian has few relationships, and we know very little about them. He has a friend called Terry, but from his few mentions of their time together, there is nothing remarkable or distinctive about their friendship – they are boys who play survival games and ride their bikes together. In another of the few relationships portrayed, there is an equal lack of complexity or depth: Brian's teacher Perpich provided some small inspiration to Brian with his ideals of positivity and motivation, but other than this we know nothing of the teacher.

The two significant relationships Brian does have are with his mother and with his father, and even those are very shadowy. We know almost nothing about Brian's father, and the main thing we know about his mother is that she had an affair ('the Secret'), which causes Brian to feel resentment and ambivalence towards her. This is encapsulated in his memory of her driving him to the airport. In the car, he 'remained silent' and doesn't answer her questions (p.6), and when he thanks her for the hatchet, he is aware that his 'words sounded hollow' (p.7). Their relationship is strained and tense, though despite 'the hot white hate of his anger at her', he is still aware that she feels 'tenderness' towards him, and in his memories of her caring for him when he was a small child we also see his fondness for her (p.7). This indicates that Brian was deeply and painfully affected by the affair and the divorce, and feels the loss of his 'normal' life acutely (p.7).

In a way, the main role of Brian's relationships with others is to amplify the sense of isolation and independence he experiences once he truly has nobody around him. In the forest, he has only himself and the natural environment.

A portrait of Brian

By exploring the areas above – actions, thoughts and relationships – we can build up a clear idea of who Brian really is, which in turn allows us to understand the themes and ideas explored in the novel.

Brian is a youthful, energetic and resilient individual who finds himself trapped in a hostile forest with no food, company or survival experience. And yet, when he recovers from the initial shock and the physical damage from the crash, he sets about finding ways to survive, learning to interpret and harness the wilderness around him, and ultimately sustaining himself with food, shelter and safety. In order to achieve this, he must be physically strong and pain-tolerant; creative and insightful; determined, stubborn and patient; and observant, perceptive and intelligent. Ultimately all these qualities add up to a character who is resilient, persistent, resourceful and able to remain optimistic despite his situation. He is also vulnerable, however, and berates himself for 'self-pity', which he sees as a weakness.

As Brian himself observes, his experience in the wilderness leads him to change in many ways. He becomes more confident, stronger, better at dealing with his thoughts and not focusing on the past, and more able to tune in to the environment around him – he becomes better at understanding the behaviour of various animals, for example. The Brian at the end of the book is not the same Brian we are introduced to at the beginning. However, aspects of Brian's characterisation in the first few chapters of the book, such as the fact that he immediately takes the initiative to fly the plane after the pilot's heart attack and makes a plan for the crashlanding, hint at the strength he possesses even early on, foreshadowing his ability to cope later in the novel. At every step of his journey, he is faced with challenges, injuries, losses, failures and fear, and it is by making it through each of these and developing survival strategies that he begins to grow and change. By the conclusion of the book, as a result of all his experiences, he has become a boy who is not fearful of his surroundings and desperate for rescue, but who (at least to some extent) enjoys his tough and solitary existence, is conflicted about the once longed-for riches in the survival pack, and is perhaps even conflicted about the arrival of the equally desired rescue plane.

Key point

In the novel's final pages, Brian retrieves the survival pack, which is filled with items that would have made his time in the wilderness so much easier. But he feels ambivalent about them – grateful and excited for some, but also uncomfortable with others such as the rifle, feeling that simply having them somehow diminishes the independent strength and resilience he has developed. This is a reminder that change and transition are never simple, but can bring both 'up and down feelings' (p.151).

Brian's parents

Key quotes

'His father was a mechanical engineer who had designed or invented a new drill bit for oil drilling …' (p.5)

'And there was the tenderness in her voice … that she had when he was small and sick, with a cold, and she put her hand on his forehead …' (p.7)

Brian's parents play only minimal roles in the text; they primarily exist to create a reason for Brian to be in the plane that crashes, and thus they unwittingly initiate his whole journey. As with the other secondary characters in this novel, we know very little about them.

His parents' divorce settlement, a month before the novel's opening, means that Brian's time will now be shared between his parents: with his mother in New York during the school year and his father in Canada in the summer holidays. He found the divorce dehumanising, with lawyers and paperwork determining his future, and his safety and comfort within his family destroyed. Most upsettingly, Brian knows – having witnessed it by chance – that his mother was seeing another man before the marriage officially fell apart. He deeply resents her for her actions, and still feels the 'hot white hate of his anger at her' when the book begins (p.7). He carries the uncomfortable weight of knowing about her infidelity ('the Secret'), unable to tell her that he knows, or to tell his father what had happened.

Despite his fury at his mother – or perhaps partly perpetuating it – he mourns for an innocent time when he was little and his mother's 'tenderness' and gentle voice meant love and safety (p.7). His memory of this childhood comfort soon fades into the background as he becomes more independent in the wilderness, but he still instinctively calls out for his mother when he poisons himself by eating too many gut cherries (p.54). This brief and even subconscious moment reminds us that at thirteen, despite his strength and resilience, he is still like a child in some ways.

We know even less of Brian's father – Brian seems to have no idea what it will be like to visit him, nor any particular excitement about seeing him.

Terry

Key quote

'I wish you were here, Terry, he thought.' (p.45)

Terry, a friend of Brian's, is a minor character who serves mainly to illustrate a chasm between Brian's past – in their carefree, make-believe game of survival in the wilderness – and his present. Their game is contrasted with Brian's experiences in the forest, where he faces the real challenges of survival alone and without the many tools they had once imagined having. We know almost nothing about Terry; he is mentioned only a few times in the novel. He acts as a reminder of Brian's recent innocence, but also shows how much Brian has learned in the short time since that naive past. As the plot progresses, Brian thinks less and less about Terry or the others in his pre-crash world.

The pilot

Key quotes

'... Jim or Jake or something, who was in his mid-forties and who had been silent as he worked to prepare for take-off.' (p.1)

'When he saw Brian look at him, the pilot seemed to open up a bit and he smiled.' (p.3)

The pilot is so insignificant a character that Brian doesn't even remember his name. This indicates how little he matters to the story; he is basically only a plot function and no more. While the scene of his heart attack is described in great detail, it is only there to facilitate the crash (and to some extent, show Brian as a boy who copes with distress by taking action), which is the inciting incident for the main plot.

Although we see the pilot as fairly gruff and withdrawn (he makes little effort at conversation with Brian), he also lets Brian fly the plane for a moment, suggesting that he does have some interest in and compassion for his young passenger. (Of course, it is also possible that part of the reason for the pilot's apparent lack of connection is that his body is beginning to respond to his upcoming heart attack.) Other than this, we learn nothing about the pilot's personality or personal history.

Perpich

Key quote

'Brian had once had an English teacher, a guy named Perpich, who was always talking about being positive, thinking positive, staying on top of things ... He was always telling kids to get motivated.' (p.39)

An old schoolteacher of Brian's, Perpich makes a few appearances in Brian's recollections of his life before the plane crash. Most notably, Brian recalls Perpich's rousing attitude and his encouragement to 'get motivated' (p.39); he was someone who cultivated positivity in his students' approach to the world. Brian has taken some of this on board and particularly embraces it in order to help him find his feet in the wilderness. He refers back to Perpich to remind himself to keep on going and to recognise his own capacity to make the situation work out. Despite being such a minor character, Perpich represents some of the key values in the text.

THEMES, IDEAS & VALUES

Resilience

Key quotes

'... stay positive and stay on top of things.' (p.39)

'... the two things, his mind and his body, had come together ... had made a connection with each other that he didn't quite understand.' (p.86)

'Nothing is that easy. Not out here, not in this place. Nothing is easy.' (p.140)

'... self-pity didn't help ...' (p.141)

For Paulsen, resilience appears to consist of two main components: psychological strength and physical strength. Without one or other of these, there is no way Brian could have survived his time in the wild. Again and again Brian experiences fear and danger, which he always shows the mental and physical capacity to overcome.

We know from the first event in the novel that even in a crisis, Brian's natural inclination is to immediately problem-solve. He thinks his way through the flying and crash-landing of the plane after the pilot's heart attack – he 'had to fly the plane. He had to help himself' (p.12) – and then drags himself from the wreckage afterwards. Paulsen celebrates this ability to stand up to danger without crumbling. Similarly, when Brian drops the hatchet in the lake, it is only for a moment that he 'felt sorry for himself' before he moves on, prioritising pragmatism over emotional responses: 'the self-pity didn't help and he knew that he had only one course of action' (p.141).

The book also links psychological strength and physical activity, showing that each interacts with the other. For example, Brian's brief but terrible emotional collapse, after the search plane doesn't see him, results in complete inactivity; he stops eating and 'let the fire go out' (p.99). On the other hand, Brian himself recognises that 'when he was busy and had something to do the depression seemed to leave' (p.84).

Key point

One advocate for resilience in Brian's pre-crash life was Perpich, who tried to instil in his students a sense of strength and agency by encouraging them to shape their own worlds and approach their experiences with positivity. It is perhaps not until Brian is forced to survive on his own that he is really able to appreciate these sentiments, and he works hard to try to put them into practice.

Mental fortitude

So much of Brian's survival, from the moment when he has to take over the flying of the plane, is not just about physical capabilities but also about mental strength and emotional resilience. He might have given up at multiple points in his journey, such as after the search plane passes by, yet he keeps going, pushing himself through trial after trial, carrying on despite his loneliness and fear. We rarely see him flailing in his determination to survive; he is driven to overcome each challenge that faces him. He sets his mind to finding practical solutions to his problems and, while his thoughts sometimes turn to his family or his friend Terry at home, he does not dwell on the fact that he is now alone. Instead, he gets on with doing whatever it is he must do at that moment – usually finding food, strengthening his shelter or refining his tools. He maintains his sanity throughout, despite having nobody to talk to and therefore no perspective beyond that of his own mind. He increasingly develops a sense of himself as being strong and capable, reaffirming his psychological hardiness.

Having mental strength, however, does not mean that one cannot experience emotional challenges. The book does not suggest that it is 'weak' to become distressed, rather it illustrates that distress is not productive and that, in order to carry on, we must be able to lever ourselves out of emotional pain and find strength again. For example, Brian has what could be described as a mental breakdown two-thirds of the way through the book when the intensity of his distress after the search plane flies away leads him to a brief period of suicidal misery, during which he 'tried to end it by cutting himself' with the hatchet (p.99). But in the morning, he awakes with a renewed mental strength, asserting that 'he would not die, he would not let death in again' (p.100). He sees this as a critical moment in his journey: he 'was not the same and would never be again like he had been' (p.100). Emerging from his deep despair, he picks himself up – stronger now – and moves on to his next challenge. In this episode we see that even mental collapse can in turn build strength.

The novel suggests that the capacity to emerge from distress is something people can only build on their own, and that mental strength is an individual quality that must be nurtured. This is symbolised by the way in which Brian, through his weeks alone, is able to survive and even thrive, while at home in his past – from the little that is shown to us – he was more dependent on others, and was deeply damaged by external events, such as his mother's affair. In the wild, through necessity, he develops independence and the vigour with which to approach difficult challenges.

Key point

At many points, Brian talks himself out of his own misery, reiterating to himself the idea that self-pity is not useful nor even acceptable; he sometimes lets himself cry briefly but sees this as something to be resisted, criticising such 'self-pity tears, wasted tears' (p.56).

Physical strength

Hatchet is a veritable catalogue of physical challenges inflicted on Brian by the environment around him. Yet no matter how damaged he is, he continues to survive. His body recovers from numerous difficulties and assaults such as:

- the mosquito swarms that attempt to devour him
- the gut cherries, which make him ill
- the moose that nearly drowns him

→

- hunger – even, early in the novel, near-starvation – and thirst
- the porcupine quills embedded in his leg
- extreme exhaustion, both chronically and (on several occasions) acutely, such as when he swims to, and then forces himself repeatedly to dive into, the wreck of the plane in the lake.

We see the incredible stress these trials place on his body. Yet, at the same time, he grows from them, and by the end of the novel he recognises himself as being a much stronger, leaner and tougher person. He sees a reflection of himself in the lake one day and observes how much his body has changed – though he also observes that 'perhaps more than his body was the change in his mind' (p.85).

Patience

Key quotes

'Patience, he thought. So much of this was patience – waiting and thinking and doing things right ... so much of all living was patience and thinking.' (p.117)

'All things come tomorrow.' (p.132)

'Patience. He was better now but impatience still ground at him ...' (p.136)

Patience, like resilience, is a quality Brian develops during his time in the wild. It is imperative for his survival, as being impatient can lead to him missing opportunities (such as when he doesn't take time to look under the surface of the water, p.87), doing himself harm (when he eats too many gut cherries at once and makes himself sick, p.54), or causing serious problems (such as when he rushes, with a 'frenzied series of hacks', to get into the submerged plane, and accidentally drops his hatchet, pp.140–1). Instead, he must learn to move at a much slower pace than he had in his previous life. He shows that he has learned patience, such as when he forces himself to ration out the turtle eggs, or when he resists attempting to dive into the plane when exhausted. He also begins to accept how long things can take in the wilderness, and is calm, for example, while waiting for the foolbirds.

Although he does not discuss it explicitly, Brian was not a particularly patient boy before the crash. One indication of this is in the phrase, 'but impatience still ground at him' (p.136) – the word *still* tells us that his impatience (although he is learning to control it) is a longstanding trait. This is an example of the impact of vocabulary choice in conveying meaning. We also see evidence of impatience in Brian's early behaviour, such as after the crash when he drinks so much water that his stomach becomes swollen – even after he tells himself that he would 'just take a sip' (p.35). Of course, this incident is driven by the immediate physical trauma of the crash, so the fact that he uncontrollably gorges water may not be purely driven by impatience. Later, even when desperately hungry, he has learned to control some of his impatience: 'I am always hungry but I can do it now' (p.119). Through necessity, he learns to cope with not immediately getting what he wants.

Ultimately, we see that Brian has learned patience, yet he still decides to treat himself to a 'feast' when he finds the survival pack (p.152). He evaluates what he has in a way that he might not have done earlier in the book: 'If I'm careful, he thought, they'll last as long as … as long as I need them to last' (p.152). He knows he will need to ration and wait. But at the same time, he 'won't be careful just yet' (p.152). This suggests that he still retains some of his earlier characteristic impatience in his urgency to devour the food; however, the 'yet' shows that he does intend to exercise care and understands the need for patience.

Determination and persistence

Patience – waiting and taking time with things – on its own is not enough to ensure Brian's survival. In addition, he must learn to be determined and persistent. So much of Brian's survival, from the first moment when he has to take over the flying of the plane, depends upon his willingness to try things over and over, and when things are not working, to change his behaviour and strategies and to again make countless attempts to get things right. He knows that if he gives up, he won't survive.

Examples of Brian's determination and persistence include his repeated attempts to meet these challenges:

- starting a fire
- gathering wood to keep the fire lit
- working out how to create and use an effective fish spear
- trying to catch the foolbirds
- rebuilding his shelter after it is destroyed by the storm
- retrieving his hatchet from the lake, and getting into the plane.

Brian does not give up, and in exchange he is rewarded with at least some degree of success. This applies at the big-picture narrative level, too: he never gives up during his time in the woods, and ultimately he is rescued.

There are also glimpses of determination and persistence in the non-human wilderness around him. For example, the moose (though with no clear purpose) does not give up when Brian escapes her attack the first time, but 'charge[s] him again … slamming him back and down into the water' (p.122). Although we don't actually know why this happens (since the moose has no need to attack him for food), clearly animals too are driven to persevere. Another example is the mosquitoes who plague him on his first night after the crash and who, as soon as his fire goes out, return again to devour him (p.126).

Maturity and growth

Key quotes

'He was new.' (p.100)

'He had changed, and he was tough. I'm tough where it counts – tough in the head.' (p.127)

'… he had a momentary loss of temper – as he would have done in the past, when he was the other person.' (p.134)

Although not strictly following all the characteristics of the genre, the novel is an example of a bildungsroman, tracing a character's journey from naivety to a kind of maturity. By definition, this genre is about growth and learning, through which wisdom may be found. For Brian, the growth is from a young boy who has led a reasonably sheltered life – 'It had always been so simple at home' (p.115) – to a boy only a little older but much wiser and stronger. With every challenge thrown at him, Brian matures just a little, eventually feeling like a completely different person from who he had been when the plane crashed. By being forced to look after himself, solely responsible for his own safety and survival, he develops a new relationship with the world around him – to the extent that, when the rescue plane finally arrives, it is he who offers food to the pilot (rather than the other way around). This symbolism is not impaired by the fact that it is pre-prepared food he did not hunt for himself; the intense effort required to get the survival pack from the sunken plane is just as demanding of his strength and survival skills as sourcing food from the forest.

The transformations that take place within Brian make *Hatchet* a coming-of-age novel. Although his maturation is not initiated by his chronological age, the series of intense events he experiences over a relatively short period of time facilitates his rapid internal growth and development.

Change and transformation

The whole book charts Brian's transition from a 'city boy' who has no idea how to find food after the plane crash to a 'tough' young man who is able to source sustenance and protect himself against wildlife and other naturally occurring threats such as the tornado. He is self-aware, able to observe the shifts in himself and to articulate what has changed. As a young adult, Brian is in a period of transition anyway, but for many protagonists around this age, the changes are slower and likely reflected in their interpersonal relationships. For Brian, the changes occur swiftly within a short period of time – his nearly two months in the wild.

The climactic shift from 'old' to 'new' Brian represents a kind of triumph over his extremely difficult circumstances. It is most notable (and most explicitly identified by Brian) following his suicide attempt. When he awakes the following morning, he 'hated what he had done to himself when he was the old Brian and was weak' (p.100), identifying a crisis point that splits his time into a before and an after. He describes himself as having 'died' and being 'born as the new Brian' (p.99) – an analogy that recalls the religious symbolism of resurrection as well as similar mythological symbolism such as that of a phoenix rising from the ashes.

The natural world

Key quotes

'… Brian knew the wolf for what it was – another part of the woods, another part of all of it.' (p.98)

'Food was simply everything … the great, single driving influence in nature.' (p.104)

'Nothing in nature was lazy.' (pp.106–7)

'… the fish he had been eating all this time had to eat, too. They had been at the pilot all this time, almost two months, nibbling and chewing …' (p.146)

Nature is really the second protagonist in *Hatchet*. The central relationship is between Brian and the wilderness around him. For the majority of the book, the natural world represents pure danger for Brian. Each and every element of the environment – be it plant, beast or climate – is out to hurt him, frighten him, threaten him, even destroy him. Despite this, Brian consistently and doggedly learns to work *with* the flora and fauna to survive and to protect himself against the dangers of the natural world. He figures out what he can eat, sometimes by trial and error (such as with the gut cherries) and sometimes by observing other animals (such as when he watches the kingfisher eat the fish and discovers a new potential source of food).

The natural world, however, is not just filled with danger and challenges to overcome – it can also be a source of awe. Occasionally, when he is not actively fighting for his life, Brian recognises the extraordinary glory of his surroundings and describes it in vivid sensory language:

> There was great beauty here – almost unbelievable beauty. The sun exploded the sky, just blew it up with the setting colour, and that colour came down into the water of the lake, lit the trees. Amazing beauty and he wished he could share it with somebody … But even alone it was beautiful … (p.137)

Man versus wild

The 'man versus wild' trope is a common one, and is a significant element of this narrative, in which Brian must battle against isolation, the elements, the natural environment around him and the animals who inhabit it. However, Brian's story is not simply one of 'triumph' over nature; it is also about finding ways to survive the wilderness through some form of alliance and harmony with it. This is evidenced, for example, when he overcomes his fear of the bear, noting that he had not been attacked just for being nearby – rather 'the bear had almost indicated that it didn't mind sharing' (p.61). It's not as though his relationships with the world around him are symbiotic: he has nothing much to offer in exchange for his survival and does of course kill animals for food. But his awareness of the interconnectedness of the wild means that he never tries to fight or kill any of the animals unnecessarily. As time passes, Brian integrates more and more into the natural world around him, becoming part of it rather than fighting against it. He feels himself developing this connection, able to 'see [and] hear differently' (p.85) and thus able to perceive subtle signs of danger as well as things that might benefit his survival.

Cycles and repetition

The book does not necessarily explore what you might think of as traditional, concrete ideas of cycles in the wild (such as birth, reproduction and death), and Brian isn't there long enough to witness the changing of the seasons, although he does start to feel the temperature beginning to drop – 'that late summer chill to the air, the smell of fall' and 'in the morning the chill was more pronounced' (p.137). Yet there is still the notion that life in the forest is cyclical. Brian's journey itself circles from one plane ride back to another, with a grand sweep of discovery and growth in between. Often his learning comes from trying something over and over and not giving up, and the repetition of his attempts to complete various activities – such as when he tries to catch the fish or the foolbirds – shows how growth, success and survival are not always linear journeys but might involve many iterations of achievements and failures.

In terms of the way the text is constructed, the repetition in the language also echoes this notion, creating rhythms of ideas, memories and feelings that are revisited until eventually they are resolved. (For more on the use of repetition in language, see 'Genre, structure & language'.)

DIFFERENT INTERPRETATIONS

Different interpretations arise from different responses to a text. Over time, a text will evoke a wide range of responses from its readers, who may come from various social or cultural groups and live in very different places and historical periods. Responses by critics and reviewers can be published in newspapers, journals and books, both online and in print. They can also be expressed in discussions among readers in the media, classrooms, book groups and so on.

While there is no single correct reading or interpretation of a text, it is important to understand that an interpretation is more than a personal opinion – it is the justification of a point of view on the text. To present an interpretation of a text based on your point of view, you must use a logical argument and support it with relevant evidence from the text.

Two interpretations

Interpretation 1: *Hatchet* shows that ultimately survival alone in the wild is unsustainable.

Again and again in *Hatchet*, we see a young city boy unable to cope in the wilderness after a plane crash of which he is the only survivor. From day one, Brian has to battle his own ignorance of his surroundings to get through each moment alive. Immediately after the crash, he knows that the only reason he is still alive is that he 'had good luck there' (p.32). He does not even know whether it will be safe to drink the water, and when he takes a gamble he drinks until he is sick. Similarly, he takes a risk on the gut cherries, again consuming far too many and making himself sick. Even at this most basic level of nourishing himself, he is helpless, and all he can think about is when a rescue plane will come for him.

His 'luck' continues throughout the text as he gradually learns more about the world around him. Certainly he fights hard in every challenge and often succeeds, such as when he persists with trying to catch fish or when he forces himself to dive (very dangerously) to retrieve his hatchet. But more often than not, his successes are due to luck. For example, he only discovers the turtle eggs because he sees the tracks by the lake, and he only escapes the moose attack because the moose randomly 'let him go this time' (p.122). Had she not done so, Brian would surely have been killed – washing his hands in the lake just before the attack was 'very nearly the last act of his life' (p.121). Perhaps most notably, Brian needs fire to keep him warm, cook meat and scare away predators, and he is unable to generate it despite his memories of people doing so in movies and television shows. It is only a pure fluke, when his hatchet hits the stone wall after he throws it at the porcupine (p.63), that he creates sparks and is then able to maintain a fire.

These numerous coincidences and convenient flukes keep Brian alive, but for how long? After many weeks in the woods, the weather begins to 'chill' (p.137), hinting at the struggles Brian would face if he was still there in the winter. Would he be able to make it through the bitterly cold weather, scarce food reserves and other challenges of the season? Perhaps so – especially if he continued to have fortunate encounters – but the text is not compelling on this.

The most significant indication that long-term survival alone in the wilderness is impossible is the fact that Brian is so desperate to retrieve the survival pack. When he does, he believes the amount of freeze-dried food inside is enough to 'last as long as … as long as I need them to last' (p.152). Yet the subtext of this line – as implied in the hesitation indicated by the ellipsis and in the word 'need' – is that he hopes he can stretch the rations out until he is rescued. Clearly, the food from the pack is *not* enough for him to live on 'for ever' (p.152). Rather, the food is a disturbing reminder of the fact that at some point Brian will begin to starve, unable to subsist on the fish, birds, rabbits and berries he has been eating so far.

The arrival of the pilot in the final pages is portrayed as such a relief to Brian that we are left believing it was ultimately only a rescue – and not his personal capabilities – that would have ensured his survival.

Interpretation 2: In *Hatchet*, even the most inexperienced city boy can step up to the challenge of survival in the wild; all it takes is determination and learning.

Brian Robeson is thirteen years old and from New York. From the moment his mother gives him a hatchet before he boards a bush plane to visit his father, he is on a journey towards independence and maturity. Even before the plane crashes, Brian is learning and growing from his experiences. He has 'never been in any kind of plane' and when the pilot offers him a turn at flying it, his response is 'I'd better not' (p.3). But with only a few moments' practice, he soon finds 'it's easy' (p.4). This foreshadows Brian's experiences throughout the book (although most involve significantly more difficulty): he begins with little knowledge of his environment or of how to live in the wild, but works hard at learning all manner of things in order to survive. He experiences many moments of uncertainty, fear, desperation, pain and frustration, but he always overcomes the challenges he faces. He is injured, faces starvation, has his shelter destroyed by a tornado and is attacked by a wild moose. It is his determination and his ability to learn that allows him to carry on despite all these incidents.

An example of Brian's growth is his increasing capacity to satisfy one of the most basic human needs: food. After the crash, Brian is starving and has no idea how he will find food:

> There was nothing obvious to eat … he hadn't seen animals to trap and cook, and even if he got one somehow he didn't have any matches so he couldn't have a fire … (p.38)

By the end of the book, however, he has comprehensively solved all these problems; through trial and error, he learns which berries are safe to eat, he catches fish, birds and rabbits, collects and eats turtle eggs, and figures out how to make a fire and keep it burning. He works hard to turn luck to his advantage, such as when he happens to find freshly laid turtle eggs and forces himself to eat them (pp.79–82) or when he 'got lucky' with a natural shelter (p.46) and works to improve it. For a city boy who knew next to nothing about wilderness survival (knowledge gleaned from films and playing with his friend Terry, p.45, was of no practical use), he has learned a great deal.

As well as learning how to feed himself, Brian constructs a shelter by building a wall to partly enclose a natural overhang. When the wall is destroyed by the tornado, Brian doesn't give up, but uses the knowledge he has gained to begin repairing it. Again, his old life had not prepared him for challenges such as this, but his problem-solving and perseverance enable him to find ways to succeed. He now knows that he can 'learn and survive and take care of himself' (p.103).

Brian also tries to 'learn from the mistakes' along the way (p.108), demonstrating that it is possible to develop confidence and skills by paying attention to past experience. Through this, he improves his ideas and techniques, thus increasing his chances of survival. A specific example is when he realises that he needs to improve the security of his shelter and keep his food safe from animals. He figures out how to weave a door for the entryway then, using the same skill, creates another door for a natural shelf on which he can store food. He is proud of what he has managed to build: 'not bad for somebody who used to have trouble greasing the bearings on his bicycle' (p.109).

This growth towards competence and ultimately survival is something Brian recognises; he often notes that he feels like a different person from the 'old' Brian before the crash. The new Brian is resilient and resourceful, and has begun to tune in to the natural environment, such as when he sees the bear (p.59) and the wolf (p.98), recognising the animals' places in the world as well as his own. He has learned to see what is around him in greater detail ('he could see things he never saw before', p.114), to evaluate danger, and to adapt in order to survive.

QUESTIONS & ANSWERS

This section focuses on your own analytical writing on the text, and gives you strategies for producing high quality responses in your coursework and exam essays.

Essay writing – an overview

An essay on a literary work is a formal and serious piece of writing that presents your point of view on the text, usually in response to a given topic. Your 'point of view' in an essay is your interpretation of the meaning of the text's language, structure, characters, situations and events, supported by detailed analysis of textual evidence.

Analyse – don't summarise

In your essays it is important to avoid simply summarising what happens in a text.

- A **summary** is a description or paraphrase (retelling in different words) of the characters and events. For example: 'Macbeth has a horrifying vision of a dagger dripping with blood before he goes to murder King Duncan.'
- An **analysis** is an explanation of the real meaning or significance that lies 'beneath' the text's words (and images, for a film). For example: 'Macbeth's vision of a bloody dagger shows how deeply uneasy he is about the violent act he is contemplating, and conveys his sense that supernatural forces are impelling him to act.'

A limited amount of summary is sometimes necessary to let your reader know which part of the text you wish to discuss. However, always keep this to a minimum and follow it immediately with your analysis of what this part of the text is really telling us.

Plan your essay

Carefully plan your essay so that you have a clear idea of what you are going to say. The plan ensures that your ideas flow logically, that your argument remains consistent and that you stay on the topic. An essay plan should be a list of **brief dot points** covering no more than half a page.

- Include your central argument or main contention – a concise statement of your overall response to the topic.
- Write three or four dot points for each paragraph, indicating the main idea and evidence/examples from the text. Note that in your essay you will need to *expand* on these points and *analyse* the evidence.

Structure your essay

An essay is a complete, self-contained piece of writing. It has a clear beginning (the introduction), middle (several body paragraphs) and end (the last paragraph or conclusion). It must also have a central argument that runs throughout, linking each paragraph to form a coherent whole. See examples of introductions and conclusions in the 'Analysing a sample topic' and 'Sample answer' sections.

The introduction establishes your overall response to the topic. It includes your main contention and outlines the main evidence you will refer to in the course of the essay. Write your introduction *after* you have done a plan and *before* you write the rest of the essay.

The body paragraphs argue your case – they present evidence from the text and explain how this evidence supports your argument. Each body paragraph needs:

- a strong **topic sentence** (usually the first sentence) that states the main point being made in the paragraph
- **evidence** from the text, including some brief quotations
- **analysis** of the textual evidence, with **explanation** of its significance and how it supports your argument
- **links back to the topic** in one or more statements, usually towards the end of the paragraph.

Connect the body paragraphs so that your discussion flows smoothly. Use some linking words and phrases such as 'similarly' and 'on the other hand', though don't start every paragraph like this. Another strategy is to use a significant word from the last sentence of one paragraph in the first sentence of the next.

Use key terms from the topic – or synonyms for them – throughout, so the relevance of your discussion to the topic is always clear.

The conclusion ties everything together and finishes the essay. It includes strong statements that emphasise your central argument and provide a clear response to the topic.

Avoid simply restating the points made earlier in the essay – this will end on a very flat note and imply that you have run out of ideas and vocabulary. The conclusion should be a logical extension of what you have written, not just a repetition or summary of it. Writing an effective conclusion can be a challenge. Try using these tips:

- Start by linking back to the final sentence of the second-last paragraph, rather than leaping back to your main contention straight away – this helps your writing to flow.
- Use synonyms and expressions with equivalent meanings to vary your vocabulary. This allows you to reinforce your line of argument without being repetitive.
- When planning your essay, think of one or two broad statements or observations about the text's wider meaning. These should be related to the topic and your overall argument. Keep them for the conclusion, since they will give you something 'new' to say but still follow logically from your discussion. The introduction will be focused on the topic, but the conclusion can present a wider view of the text.

Essay topics

1 'The hatchet is the most important thing in the novel.'
To what extent do you agree?

2 How does Paulsen explore the idea of resilience?

3 'The central conflict in *Hatchet* is between Brian and his own weaknesses.'
To what extent do you agree?

4 What does *Hatchet* say about the relationship between humans and the natural world?

5 'Brian only survives in the wilderness because of luck.'
To what extent do you agree?

6 "… he learned the most important rule of survival, which was that feeling sorry for yourself didn't work." Discuss.

7 How does Paulsen use repetition to develop the themes in *Hatchet*?

8 "The pack was wonderful but it gave him up and down feelings."
How do Brian's emotions shape his survival?

9 What is the impact of vivid imagery in this novel?

10 "… even alone it was beautiful …"
What does *Hatchet* say about loneliness?

Vocabulary for writing on *Hatchet*

Anorak: a kind of jacket.

Bildungsroman: a literary genre in which the narrative revolves around the development of a character, usually through significant life events and relationships, towards maturity.

Food fish: the name Brian gives to the fish he eats from the lake.

Foolbirds: Brian's name for the small birds he eventually learns to catch for food.

Forest/woods: a natural landscape that predominantly features trees. Although the terms 'forest' and 'woods' are similar to the Australian word 'bush', the three are not always interchangeable – bush is generally specific to Australian wilderness areas. You should use the North American language to describe the landscape in this text, since that is the environment being discussed. Other terms you could use to vary your descriptions and reduce repetition include the wild or wilderness, and the natural environment.

Gut cherries: Brian's name for the first berries he eats in the forest, which make him ill.

Hatchet: a kind of axe that has a short handle and is small enough to use with one hand.

Analysing a sample topic

"He had changed, and he was tough."
How much do you think Brian has changed by the end of the novel?

There are many forms of essay topics. Some include a direct quote from the novel (as this topic does) while others make a statement about the text and then provide you with a prompt such as 'Do you agree?' or 'Discuss'. Some topics ask a direct question, such as 'How does Paulsen explore the idea of resilience?'

Although your essay structure (as discussed in 'Essay writing – an overview' above) will remain the same no matter the topic, your argument and your approach to analysing the topic and the text might vary. For example, when a prompt asks you to 'discuss' a statement, you do not need to strongly agree or disagree with the statement, but rather you should explore evidence and viewpoints around it. You might start by gathering all the quotes you can find that are related to the statement, and then group them into different categories such as setting, character and conflict. You can use these groups as the basis for your paragraphs.

For an agree/disagree topic, you will need to create your main contention – a statement summarising your response to the topic – before drafting your essay. One way of doing this is to brainstorm ideas relating to the topic, find evidence in the text to support your ideas (quotations, events etc.) and then divide the evidence into two columns: one supporting an argument that agrees with the topic, and the other supporting an argument that disagrees with the topic. You can then see which argument you think has more evidence to support it.

A broader topic like the one on page 61 gives you more freedom to explore ideas, but you must still make sure that you evaluate the information in the topic and focus on a central argument. This topic does not ask you to agree or disagree, but the question hints that your main contention should support or refute the statement in the quotation. Here, for example, your contention might be: 'Although Brian matures during his time in the wilderness, he had the strength to survive all along – it just took the challenges of isolation to bring it to the fore.' This contention responds to the 'how much' element in the topic by arguing that Brian experiences *some* change, but does not change *completely*. Other key terms in this topic you should pay attention to include:

- the character name (your essay will focus on a character, rather than narrative elements and techniques)
- the direct quotation (make sure you understand it and know its context, including where it appears in the text)
- the phrase 'by the end of the novel' (this directs you to the way you should approach your argument – by looking at Brian's journey as a whole).

Make sure you respond to *all* the key elements in a topic, not just one or two of them.

Sample introduction

> *Hatchet* is a coming-of-age novel about a city boy who survives a plane crash, then – improbably – survives on his own in the wilderness for nearly two months, thanks to his resilience, determination and problem-solving abilities. While his time in the woods helps him to mature, become independent and increase his physical strength, his ability to do so derives from qualities that he already had. These attributes were merely latent, as his life had never required him to call on them. It is through his quick thinking and persistence that he first survives the crash, and these same qualities enable him to survive right up until his rescue.

Body paragraph outline

Paragraphs 1 and 2: Begin by acknowledging some of the ways in which Brian has changed, supporting your points with quotations or direct evidence.

- He has become physically stronger and leaner – 'he noticed that his body was changing. He had never been fat, but he had been slightly heavy ... This was completely gone and his stomach had caved in to the hunger' (p.85).
- His problem-solving skills have improved – 'not bad for somebody who used to have trouble greasing the bearings on his bicycle' (p.109).
- He has learned patience – while he gorges himself on berries early in the novel, by the end he knows to pace himself; for example, he waits until the next day to take the raft to the plane after building it.

Paragraph 3: Move on to describe the ways in which Brian has *not* changed.

- He already had the mental resilience to survive, recalling lessons Perpich had taught him long ago: 'You are your most valuable asset' (p.40).
- He is as determined and as competent at the beginning of the novel as he is at the end. Just as he persists at building the raft and diving for the survival pack towards the end of the narrative, in the first chapters he takes over the flying of the plane, despite having no experience, and puzzles out a way to make a landing that would give him the best chance of survival.
- Many of his triumphs are due to luck rather than growth or maturation on his part. For example, he happens upon the tracks leading to the turtle eggs, and it's only by accident that he creates sparks that allow him to start a fire.

Paragraph 4: Compare the evidence you presented in the previous paragraphs to show which side of the discussion you find more compelling. This will lead you to your conclusion, where you can explicitly state your response to the 'how much' question in the topic.

- Brian himself reiterates the fact that he has changed, noting that he has developed greater psychological resilience (become 'tough in the head', p.127) and patience, and sees the world differently.
- The narrative shows him learning about his surroundings and navigating his challenges with persistence (such as when he repeatedly tries to catch the fish, and eventually does).
- However, he was tough, smart and independent from the beginning. As well as taking command of the crashing plane, after the crash he immediately, once he is physically able, takes stock of what he has and what he must do, refuses to give in to despair and tells himself to 'get motivated' (p.40).

- He becomes more competent during his journey, but only by developing skills specific to his new surroundings, such as figuring out how to catch the foolbirds (by looking for their shapes) or realising that he needs to store food. These are practical developments that don't change Brian's intelligence or problem-solving ability.
- The Brian at the end of the book knows how to *do* many more things than the Brian of the first pages, but he is still the same Brian.

Sample conclusion

> Although by the end of *Hatchet* Brian has become physically stronger, has more patience and has learned much about survival, most of his qualities – his problem-solving abilities, determination, self-awareness and independence – were in fact there from the beginning. Being forced to stay alive on his own in a hostile environment revealed these characteristics. By the end of the novel, Brian is still essentially the same boy, but he has learned to apply and make the best of his existing personal assets and capabilities.

SAMPLE ANSWER

'The hatchet is the most important thing in the novel.' To what extent do you agree?

The hatchet, which Brian's mother gives him before the fateful flight intended to take him to stay with his father, is central to Brian's survival: 'Without the hatchet he had nothing … was nothing. The hatchet was, had been him.' It is nearly the only object of any use that he has with him when the plane crashes; the tool, which he had initially only put on his belt to 'humour' his mother, becomes his most prized possession. However, the hatchet is primarily something that facilitates Brian's own resourcefulness and determination, qualities that are far more important than any physical object.

In an environment in which Brian has to fight ceaselessly to survive, the hatchet is a tool that can serve many purposes, and 'the only weapon' he has. He uses it to chop wood and make other tools (the spear and the bow); to cut into the side of the plane; and to make fire. In this sense, the hatchet is vital during Brian's time in the wilderness. Often, though, it is subservient to his own capabilities as he becomes better at surviving. For example, the hatchet does not enable him to find the raspberries or the turtle eggs, and although it does allow him to cut wood for fuel, for the spear and for the ladder to his food storage, these are tasks that Brian has devised independently – the hatchet merely makes the jobs easier and more efficient. He might have been able to break up wood in other ways, but he uses the tool he happens to have with him.

As well as being important on a practical level, the hatchet is a powerful symbol representing a number of ideas. Firstly, it signals that he carries his past with him and, as such, he carries pain, because it is directly linked to both his mother's infidelity and his parents' separation. Though he rarely considers it this way, it is a permanent reminder of his life before the crash; it echoes the time when he was supported externally and lived in an environment with tools and resources immediately available to him. Secondly – in a slightly contradictory way – the hatchet is a symbol of his growing capacity to protect and sustain himself in a hostile environment. He becomes, like his hatchet, 'tough where it counts'. As a weapon, the hatchet is also a symbolic reminder of the extreme dangers of the wild, and has the capacity to cause violent injury in just as aggressive a way as the porcupine, the moose or the tornado.

Although Brian generally benefits from the hatchet, on one significant occasion he uses it in a negative way. In desperation after the first search plane fails to see him, he deliberately cuts himself with it, intending to commit suicide – 'he wanted to die'. In this sense, the hatchet also symbolises the fine line between danger and success, between death and survival. It is a tool that can wound as well as protect. The binary reflects Brian himself: able to use his intelligence and strength to stay alive in extraordinary circumstances, yet also his own worst enemy at times when he is consumed by doubts, desolation and hopelessness.

Finally, Brian's hatchet is a symbol of the constant challenge of surviving in the wilderness. At a climactic point in the novel, not long before he is finally rescued, he accidentally drops his hatchet into the lake. This could have spelled the end of his time in the forest, as he has come to feel dependent on the tool. Giving up and letting it go would symbolise a hopelessness that he has, for the most part, refused to surrender to – he repeatedly insists that 'self-pity didn't help'. Instead, he makes an almost superhuman (and successful) effort to retrieve the tool, showing simultaneously how dependent upon it he is, and yet also how resilient, determined and strong he has become.

While the hatchet is a vital survival tool for Brian, it is not the only thing that keeps him alive. It supplements and reinforces his own resourcefulness and determination and the fact that, as Brian puts it while recalling the lessons of his old teacher Perpich, 'I'm all I've got.'

REFERENCES & READING

Text

Paulsen, G 2017, *Hatchet*, Macmillan, London. First published 1987.

References and other resources

American Writers Museum 2021, 'A conversation with Gary Paulsen, author of *Gone to the Woods*', 14 January, YouTube, https://www.youtube.com/watch?v=TXio0YvnXZc

Balaban, S 2021a, 'Beloved children's author and wilderness enthusiast Gary Paulsen has died at 82', *All Things Considered*, 14 October, https://www.npr.org/2021/10/14/1045981769/gary-paulsen-hatchet-author-obituary

Balaban, S 2021b, 'Gary Paulsen's memoir taps into the childhood experiences that inspired his stories', *Weekend Edition Saturday*, 17 April, www.npr.org/2021/04/17/988331566/gary-paulsens-memoir-taps-into-the-childhood-experiences-that-inspired-his-stori

Sides, AG 2006, 'On the road and between the pages, an author is restless for adventure', *The New York Times*, 26 August, https://www.nytimes.com/2006/08/26/books/on-the-road-and-between-the-pages-an-author-is-restless-for-adventure.html